AF606860

PROPERTY OF

ART OF NATURE

# BOTANICAL COLLECTION

INSIGHTS

*an imprint of*

INSIGHT EDITIONS

www.insighteditions.com



MANUFACTURED IN CHINA

10 9 8 7 6 5 4 3